WITH SOME WILD WOMAN

Jill Gardiner is a former Chair of Brighton Poets. Her poetry has been published in *The North*, the *Western Mail*, *The Interpreter's House*, *Artemis* and various anthologies, and won prizes in the Cardiff International and the Kent & Sussex Poetry Society competitions. She has read her work at the Poetry Café in London, the Sanctuary Café in Hove, the Sussex Arts Club in Brighton, and at Wine, Women and Words in Skala Eressos, Lesvos.

As a historian, Jill has appeared at Kenric nights, and at Polari Literary Salons at the Southbank Centre and the Marlborough Theatre, Brighton. Her book *From the Closet to the Screen: Women at the Gateways Club 1945-85* is published by Rivers Oram / Pandora. The *Observer* described it as 'fascinating and sometimes hilarious'.

This is her first poetry collection.

WITH SOME WILD WOMAN

POEMS 1989–2019

Jill Gardiner

To Peggy and Alison,

All good wishes,

Jill Gardiner

Tollington

First published in 2019 by Tollington Press, Machynlleth, Wales, UK
www.tollingtonpress.co.uk

Copyright © Jill Gardiner 2019
The moral right of the author has been asserted.

A catalogue record for this book is available from the British Library.

ISBN 978-1-909347-16-8

Printed and bound in Wales by Y Lolfa, Talybont, Ceredigion, on FSC-certified paper

FSC

Contents

4. travelling on

For you, sweetheart, with much love.
Still surprising and delightful after all these years...

Foreword

Many of these poems are about romantic love. Some are also erotic, or humorous, or both. Love is problematic when you discover, growing up, that your passions are often awoken by other women. We still live in a society where, despite millions of us experiencing same-sex attraction, such freedom to love is not always fully understood or actively encouraged. Yet love against the odds still has a universal human appeal.

This collection starts with a prize-winning poem, about adoration from afar in an earlier era, to remind us that these feelings have always existed. Then we embark on 'the path to love', which follows, in the order in which events unfolded, how the poet found her way to expressing her feelings and having them returned. It starts with childhood crushes, the impact of puberty, and the search for identity and happiness – including the discovery of Bohemianism from French writers. Then a series of poems, some lyrical and some entertaining, celebrate mutual love and attraction, ending with a sequence on a long-term relationship, and how it remains erotic.

The 'beacons' section reflects the way that once we've found a partner, we tend to open out with curiosity to the wider world. Through myth, painting, history and biography, it explores various creative, daring or inspiring women and men. It's followed by 'love and loss', which focuses on family, from childhood memories to mid-life observation of later-life experiences (including illness and death). It pivots around the meeting of two worlds. The poet leaves after Sunday lunch, not without comment from her relations, to go to a wedding between two men, in the days when same-sex partners created their own ceremonies, before even civil partnerships were legalised. 'Travelling on' concludes with the themes of emotional recovery from loss, and of the joy of voyaging beyond home, including to the birthplace of the poet Sappho, and to the recent marriage of two women in France, where love has often been celebrated in relative freedom.

1. the path to love

At the Opera

(after the painting by Mary Cassatt)

I have seen her each night from afar
Across a salon, or in some distant room
And often on his arm. And, tonight,
I have followed her to the opera.
In the picture, you do not see her:
Her bare shoulders; the three strings
Of pearls I gave her; the shock
Of that white muslin dress in November.

You only see me in my tight black gown,
And my opera glasses fixed on some point
Beyond your sight, and the yellowing fan
I am hardly holding. Any moment now
My grip will tighten as she turns
From him and catches my eye again.
One time she blushed. We are rarely alone.
Our intimacy is confined to public places.

In a distant box, you see another man:
Where I go, he follows. And grown so bold
That his opera glasses are trained on me
As if that whole wide audience were not there.
I have heard them whisper in the drawing rooms:
'She's handsome still, and alone too long.
Why does he wait?' He has asked. I freeze.
I am spoken for and cannot say to whom.

The Long Voyage to the West End

The lights go down. The orchestra lets rip.
I don't do musicals. Well now I do:
attracted by the cast, I made the trip,
a Boho in the back seats, waiting for you.

The first half passes. Then it's burlesque.
You play a stripper, an Amazon in gold.
You're thrusting for laughs. They adore you too.
Your voice is raunchy and you're oh! so bold.

You once played the lead, on our old school stage:
no helmet crushed your cloud of auburn hair.
Bewitching us as Circe, nine years of age,
your solo voice erupted like a flare

igniting my six-year-old heart. To us
your voice was Carmen and Callas.
'For I'm a witch!' 'Yes, she's a witch!' we'd chorus.
Off-stage you ran barefoot across the grass

and freckles followed. You grew tall, typecast
as 'character', so versatile with voice.
To me you're the star who silenced a hall
and launched me into love. I had no choice.

The Long Voyage of Odysseus was a school musical play.

14

Ten

Pamela Redburn's bosoms have grown!
She's the talk of the class, she's the only one.
I wish I had bosoms like Pamela Redburn's,
Pamela Redburn's bosoms have grown.

Her mother refuses to buy her a bra
'cos she's only ten and far too young
but oh, Mrs Redburn, why can't you see
how enormous Pamela's bosoms are?

You weren't there on the field today:
Miss Geare shouted, 'Run!' and Pamela groaned.
She kept at the back, how slowly she ran:
her bosoms were bouncing up and down.

They wobble. It's wonderful. I roll my vest
right up over that bit of my chest
so they might think I've got bosoms too:
under my blouse – size thirty-two.

Mandy prods me. No one's fooled
but some of them roll up their vests too.
We all want bosoms like Pamela Redburn's:
soft and pale and round and new.

She says: we can have them. The boys are a pain,
calling rude words out again and again;
but we still want bosoms like Pamela Redburn's.
Pamela Redburn's bosoms have grown.

My First Bra

came in Christmas paper. Lacy,
lilac. Uncle Harry whistled.
My mother offered the aunts
a private view. We slipped
upstairs, all girls together.
Harry offered to lend a hand
but my father stopped his mouth
with a Churchill cigar.

The expert aunts slipped hooks
into place; giggled over battle-plates
they used to wear in wartime,
and Granny, who kept comfy
in no bra at all, remember?
At last: something to show off
in the changing room. 'Padded?
Course not. Cross my heart.'

When Sally takes a shower
hers jiggle: you could juggle them.
We have to share a cubicle:
it always makes me blush.
Our backs against cold walls,
Sally glaring, me not staring.
Are mine still a pair of pimples
that no one longs to touch?

Chemistry Lesson

She lit the magnesium. Sun-bright, its flare
enlightened my heart. All gods grew dim and died.
White-robed priestess, with half-moon fingernails,
her chemistry taught me more than she knew:
licensed for explosions, teacher with a rebel grin,

she flirted with fathers at parents' evenings,
and charmed their weary wives. I remained
mute and marvelling, learning her by heart:
for what could I declare in my school blazer,
granny glasses and sensible shoes?

Denuded of jewellery, booted on the hockey field
muddily, we grunted up and down. Pubescent
bodies bored me, but my teacher's alchemy
I chronicled in unshared poetry,
hidden underneath the carpet every night.

At the charity cake sale, the music was booming,
girls howling that they can't survive without love.
I knew then the feeling, but not what to do with it.
Contrary to hearsay, most adults weren't up for it,
and no women at all, so far as I knew.

Had I only known where to go. To Chelsea,
through gateways she never entered, where you,
love of my life, were so at home. The jukebox,
the women, the staircase, the eyes. I got there later.
Yet what a waste of my green and yearning years!

French Exchange
(Ghazal for Karen)

When we were young, you took us to that turquoise sea:
where mimosa bloomed and lemons grew, that turquoise sea.

By day, we soaked up sun, turned gold or seasoned pine
among the topless bathers who knew that turquoise sea.

I devoured Sagan, learned Baudelaire by heart,
when sand was red-hot, love still new. That turquoise sea!

We'd share Camembert, fresh baguette, ripe *abricots*,
knock back cider, then run into that turquoise sea.

Forbidden subjects aired, among the olive trees,
we grew bold: owed it all to you, that turquoise sea.

At night, we drank rosé de Provence, learned to waltz,
while liquid lights streamed fire through that turquoise sea.

Today we wheel you to the sun-soaked park. You bask,
words all gone. Do you miss it too, that turquoise sea?

I would give every book I own, my unlived days,
to dance with you, above that view, that turquoise sea.

My Mother's Gift

I didn't choose the coat
but she adored it:
brown, tweed, midi,
and the fit was perfect.
I thanked her, best I could
and asked what she'd worn
to go up to university.

Her navy surplus suit,
that saved on ration coupons.
Americans sent parcels,
and she picked that ticket:
for a rich red cardigan,
making her the envy
of all the other girls.

I tried to like the coat
but never felt myself in it:
so sneaked off to sell it
in a secondhand shop
where someone stole it.
So others shared her view
and I never got the money.

But I was all smiles
in a man's black jacket –
recycled DJ with wide lapels –
stomping through bronzed leaves,
smoking Gitanes,
with Sartre and de Beauvoir
on my bedside table.

She must have noticed
but she never said a word.

Bridges

I built myself a turret – stone solid thick.
Am safe inside. Mountain stretches down
below. I watch valleys where people
hold hands together in the open sun.
Used to go out to play with them
but could not live to their horizons, so

cut off and ran.
                    Built myself a tower, nine to five
in which to keep myself alive.

But I did not bargain for you, on some far peak
actually building bridges, their ropes
swaying a little, it is true; but bridges,
still bridges, some stretching right the way down
to the valley I had left behind.

And now I really do not know what to do
with this bridge materialising between me and you:
if you were not blind, you would know the gulf unbridgeable.
If my turret were secure, I would not even see you.

Building bridges is a dangerous business:
a plank or two loose-fitted and we may fall through,
and even if the construction should be sound, who knows
how swaying together may unbalance me and you?

Bee Orchid

From the meadow path before us lie
expanses of uninterrupted green.
Yet here, fresh earth upon the grass:
a badger's sett beneath our solid ground.

On the slope, a piece of slate: you lift it
and there lies the slow-worm, pale, unexpected –
snake-like, yet not a snake at all.

This path itself:
till today I did not know
it lay so close to home.

Here you brought me in search of an orchid
that only flowers for a single day:
it bobs like a bee on a delicate bloom.

There are bees, yes, weighing down the buttercups;
orchids too, fragile, magenta against the green,
but bee orchids? None.

I cannot tell you the relief I feel
that the hidden is still concealed;
that the more we discover,
the more lies waiting
behind the surfaces of things.

The Encyclopaedia of Sexual Knowledge

The only way to find real information then,
it lurked discreetly on a bottom shelf
of my father's endless book collection.
Lady Chatterley hadn't been much help,
read by torchlight under rose-pink blankets.
Nor had what Biology had taught us
of rabbits, humans, penis inserted
into vagina, pregnancy, full stop.

But in these illuminating, well-read pages
I discovered frottage and paraphilia,
what women did with women, men with men.
Yet love poems still remained the vital guide
to those silent feelings I couldn't share
which filled the room when that person was there.

Les Amies

You parted your lips, and out flowed Paris:
the slopes of Montmartre led us all the way.
Piaf pervaded your leafy London terrace
where we would lounge with *cafés allongés*,
laugh, kiss deep: your *vin* never *ordinaire*.
Discussion of Anaïs Nin might ensue,
or of women we'd loved, with cascading hair,
which rooftop had once been yours, in that view.

Too cool to be sketched on the Place du Tertre,
or to haunt the Lapin Agile cabaret,
the passion in your violet-ink letters,
and what your flesh could do, carried me away.
I was your English rose with long blonde hair.
Your voice was enough to transport me there.

Since I've grown to know you, I find cattle fascinate me

Out walking, I am halted
by wedge heads, rising,
their mouths alone mobile
in circular motion.

When life still promised lightning,
how I despised their cud-dull lives!
Yet years have enlarged their eyes
to shock me. Their lashes curl
like those of girls. Eyes
on all sides stare through me.

A speech seems expected.
'Unaccustomed to cows as I am...'
Well, you know how I blush.
They contemplate me calmly.
Oh to be a cow! You know where you stand.

One alone of the herd, advancing,
like a lumbering boulder could do for me.
What a monument you might make of me:
'Crushed by curious cows, she died.'

Then just as I dare to prepare to caress one
they turn. Their haunches rippling,
the broad-backed bulk of them swaying,
away they glide like whales across an open sea,
parting the grass before them.

Theirs is a gradual, unfamiliar grace.
Absurdly, I try walking at their pace
but cannot match it quite.
You could. Wish you were here.

To Another Poet

By day her hair was plaited tight.
We swapped our poems, read and read.
The hours passed. No word was said.
She let her hair flow loose at night.

When we went out the moon took fright,
pulled down a veil and hid behind.
Paths later, we'd lost track of time,
it smelt so green. Her hand felt right.

The sky cleared, the leaves turned white
and she reached out towards the moon,
remembered the stream, much further on,
longed to go there and watch the light.

It felt too far, so, quite contrite
I kissed her, turned and led her back.
Some other poet will draft a villanelle
about unloosening her hair each night.

Yet we found the haiku we had to write
sheltered behind the curtain of her hair:
by day she wore it plaited tight,
but she let it all flow loose that night.

Celibacy

Out of the shower you came: damp, laughing, pink,
and, under a wrap-around towel, quite nude.
'We're both girls: what the hell!' I didn't blink.
You lay down in your knickers. I looked: was that rude?

You said you didn't want a lover, not today,
(on our first night in Paris, you alone with me...)
but if you did, she'd be French, or foreign anyway
(so I'd have to be resigned to celibacy).

So I was. I saw your point: sex after all
tangles the threads of the neatly woven life,
makes you oversleep when your mother's due to call,
inspires some to deceive their current wife.

No sex: fine with me. But then this Parisienne appeared
on the Rue Mouffetard, where the buskers played:
bronzed, chic, slim, she caught my eye, she stared.
'Vous aimez les femmes?' I stared. 'Bien sûr!' I said.

She said I had the charm of an English rose
and gave me a caress that left me blinking
at a woman whose experience was no pose...
'What's she on about? Here! She's winking!'

Oh fantasy made flesh! I could have wept
as I left, with you teasing me all the way
back: 'Vous aimez les femmes?' When you slept
she invaded my dreams and I didn't run away.

So how did it happen? That next week in Brighton
you gave me that long look I didn't dare
give you. We even left the light on.
What did it, you said, was all that sea air.

Monk's House, Rodmell

Place imprinted with larger-than lives:
Mrs Woolf to you, the principal ghost.
Here still is the virgin-narrow bed,
the white-lace counterpane she selected,
Angelica Garnett's ice-bright daffodils
chastely placed beside Virginia's bed.

'It's all green paint in there,' you say,
and stretch, lazy upon grass.
Clean as a cat, your long slim body
bathed in the evening before,
the morning after making love.
'And a naked lady hanging by her door...

Did Vita come here? Bet Vita
came everywhere, like you and me.
Don't you dare! People'll see.
Get your hands off, sexpot!
I'm such a closet, me. And your
students' eyes could be anywhere.'

I pose you by the statue letting loose
her robes across one breast:
it's so like your breast, I caress it.
So here you're imprinted, someone's memory.
Behind the trees, where they'd have gone,
we leave one long kiss.

Valentine

you
offered me
half the moon
in   a   half-past-
midnight   sky.   I
wasn't half tempted
but we were half-cut
at the time and only
half-inclined   to
remember your
other
h
a
l
f

walk on the wild side

Mostly I've walked on the safe side all my life:
it comes of being born too late to lie
in Hyde Park handing daisies to passers-by.
By my time, the hippies had Habitat homes
and the yuppies sat with their portable phones
and lunched on champagne, Chinese leaf and prawns.

So mostly I've walked on the safe side all my life:
here I am with my job, my flat, my answerphone.
There are you, stripped pine and paintings at home,
but you were there then, that's the difference.

Meeting you reminds me of how I used to dream
of a break from the rat-race to run away to Spain,
busk on beaches, pick oranges, drift home,
smoke pot, talk to tramps, doss around,
write poetry all day, stay up all night
and talk of Kafka, coke, Kama Sutra
and your eyes
                your eyes mostly.

The way we danced last night was on the wild side:
not hand in hand but cheek to cheek, breast to breast.
Well I'd always known I fancied you,
when you suddenly said you fancied me too.

A sealed jar has cracked
and life has flooded through:
you've woken me to what I want to do
with some wild woman.

What a drag
it can't be you.

it wasn't on the map, the place you wanted me to see

so we drive off anyway, following the names
of the nearest villages you remember
on roads that might reach our destination.
We know we'll arrive. Confidence comes
with the smiles we exchange
mile by mile as the signposts pass.

The Downs have never grown so green.
Mad as March, our first spring day.

We circle the lanes for a half hour or two.
Each naked branch is now unfurling
and the bluebells are all in bloom.
Old beech leaves shrivel against the new
and the trees frisk the roof of the car
as we pass. Lanes narrow: country, deep.
We smile, eye to eye, again,
your hand seeking mine all the way.

You half feel, half remember, where to go.
I love you when we miss the road and you are calm.
You love me as I go into a pub to ask the way.

We arrive. Your land, at last.

Here is the stable. Look. The half door.
There will be a wood-burning stove over here,
there a window enlarged. On the terrace
that will be here, we could breakfast
in sun. Down there is a fresh spring stream.
Here will be orchards. Look at their beginning:
three trees, down there, the blossom swelling.
Cuckoo. Cuckoo. The first. Do you hear?

Look. Those primroses. All in flower.

Here things grow, are fine if left to be.

Like young girls we sit in the long grass for hours
that do not pass. Dream dreams, sow seeds:
talk for all day and all night and tomorrow.
There are silences too, like earth after rain.

Below is a meadow. Beyond, a hill.

Here it is as simple as this:
your eyes, my eyes, the sun,
a day of unaccounted hours.

And only when I leave you alone
do I find violets flinching
against fresh grass, and wonder:
how did I come here?

A chaffinch flash of wings.

There is no going back
for all roads lead this way:
it's it and it's you and it's here.

Wigan Weekends

The first time I wanted to prove it,
woke in the night and had to reach out
to be sure this gentle breathing was you.
Pinched myself, pulled back again,

went soft as a sand-dune at the way
you snored. Felt your warmth
across the gap, between chaste beds
we'd pushed together, would ease apart

by day. Late for breakfast, down the Pier,
two strong coffees in the Orwell Tavern,
snatched some photos, preserved us there,
hesitant or half-asleep, each of us alone

which is not how we remember it at all:
the muddy path that leads across the moors,
grass turning gold, your fingers searching
for mine. Daring to kiss in the open air.

At dinner we wrangle happily for hours,
smoothly gliding against each other's lives
as, in bed later, our warm wet bodies do.
No promises, none. We choose each other.

Late for Dinner

So long since breakfast.
Your fingers part me like a
peach. Juice flows and flows.

Not Over Yet

Then, it rained natterjack toads
and mountain ranges sprang up in the middle
of motorways. Flats collapsed like scenery.
Cut glass sang as it sliced through fingers.
The earth split its skin; dust flew
in the face of the sun. It was an eclipse.
There was nowhere to go.

I tried mandragora, meditation, mayhem:
nothing chased disaster away.

Now, peonies bloom from the carpets,
orangutans swing from chandeliers and
candles flicker from every window in town.
It was an awakening, a re-awakening
when the embers shifted under all that dust.
The city arose from the ashes as we kissed
and a car revved up along the open road.

I could spend all day simply looking at you.
Preston Park is full of roses.

Chess Game

Shall we play chess or go to bed?
We can't make up our minds
so you get the chess set,
I fetch the wine, and we both
slip out of our clothes.

This bed is big enough for all of us:
you, propped up on a pillow
too far away to reach:
between us, queens and kings,
their armies of retainers.

A clock ticks. Your pawns advance.
My knight prepares to pounce.
The curve of your hip. Two moves
and I'll have you in check. Too late.
What is your bishop doing down there?

You tell me I'm beautiful: this is not
the time, now you've swiped my pawn,
gone up a piece. Oh your skin
and you so at ease in it
as if you went naked everywhere.

I must concentrate, this is serious.
Your breath so close, your body
out of reach. I could stretch...
You must be joking. Not my queen.
Your breasts. I resign, I concede.

Before We Met

I never did have sex when I should.
You had it everywhere, all the time.

My room was dark, with poems suspended:
romantic negatives, always undeveloped.

Some woman glanced at you across the room:
tonight's moth circling your cool blue flame.

The blinds were down at my frosted window:
each solitary bath a sub-erotic dream.

You pulled the curtains inside your car,
kept a reputation – she today, tomorrow her.

I was faithful to a dream of a woman I adored
while some guy gripped her thighs, oblivious.

Here and now, you could have anyone, but don't.
I, who never slept around, am slippery with wanting you

each way, this way, now. You hold tight.
We cry out. I could weep. You tell me

this is making love, and nothing like the other.
However did we meet? Incredible. Such bliss.

Summer Night

(after the painting by Winslow Homer)

They strain to see the lovers walk along the sand,
first to see: are they beautiful? Does her
tumbling hair frame a face like those they've loved?
Is that hand in her back pocket or around her waist?

In summer, there are lovers all over the place,
shooting up like lilies into sudden bloom.
Long brown legs, my, hasn't she grown?
It's all that rain we've been having, all that sun,

that barbecue down on the beach that did it.
The gulls called. The waves broke. Someone laughed.
There was a look that lasted. And then they danced:
an arm on her shoulder, her cheek so close, the moon.

Their bodies speak: 'How close feels right?' 'Like this.
Let's dance down there.' Yes, well away from here
where rapt shadows sit, watching in the dark.
There is a cave no one else will ever find.

They say: 'How good it is to see two women
so in love. I remember... but it was so long ago.'
Besides it's time to leave, time to douse the fire down.
A sudden cormorant dives into the deep.

Dining Out

In a vintage photo-book a friend has given me,
a crowd of 'Fifties women we'd love to meet:
shoulder to shoulder, in ties and trilbies, lipstick,
they're beaming: 'Cheese!' Their fags are glowing.
There's a forest of bottles, on a white-cloth table,
and a goblet of chocolates is circulating.

Women like us have always found a way.
Some eyes just met. Arm in arm they promenaded.
They'd grin at the attendant in the petrol station,
wiping her hands on her clean brown overalls;
or admire the pinkie ring on the usherette's finger.
The name of 'that club' was whispered, ear to ear.

And here we are tonight, in our fancy best:
a beret, a fedora, two dresses, linen trousers,
a waistcoat, you in stripes, my silk scarf flowing,
at the Hotel du Vin, where the waiter's attentive
and doesn't bat an eyelid when the girls start chanting,
demanding that we dance the Gateways Grind for them.

We may have it all now from Gaydar to marriage:
you pick up the iPad and film without asking,
the shirts are open-necked, the couples dancing,
but nothing beats a party in a private room,
where, family of choice, we can let our hair down,
and know we're loved, whatever. Just like then.

Artist's Model

There still hangs, on my wall, my one-time self:
naked as a swan, my back turned to you,
stretched out in comfort on the artist's couch,
long legs clenched together, eyes on the view.

What you don't see: the robe she handed me,
the screen to change behind, my current book.
While her charcoal went wild drawing my feet,
her girlfriend was downstairs, dying to look.

You had vanished, distracted by your past
although we still had passion in our sights.
Our love absorbed my flesh. You'd go to stay,
slip into our friend's studio at nights

to gaze on this portrait, as we now do
from this queen-sized bed, shared only with you.

Desire at Our Age

Now it's like a grasshopper
leaping through the air
that we have to chase
through long grass
while it's still there.

Long-term Relationship

You turn to me, present, suddenly real,
your screen-time, at last, exploded and gone.
My book drops away, you're making me feel
this might be the moment to abandon
all other distractions, to favour one
we mustn't forget, so tried and tested.
My lips explore yours, still second to none.
You finger my cheeks, strip me bare-breasted

as you have done a thousand times before
yet each time there's that shiver of surprise:
cuddle or seduction, we still want more
without expecting which – love's made us wise.
This close, this naked, going with the flow
we shoot the rapids. Amazed it's still so.

2. beacons

Icons

The poet of poets kissed my cheek.
I shan't wash my face all week.

Imagine you'd not simply seen her
but caught a ball hit by Martina

or the dyke in shades in HMV
had grinned at you and *was* k.d.

You're far too cool to ever say
but I know it would make your day.

Penelope Confides in Her Loom

I did plead with him not to go
but you know how he is. All these men
here in Ithaca, give them a sword
and they think they're gods.
I'd rather feel the thrust of him
inside me, the rise of the storm
in my bed, than sit and sing of him
gone off sailing, intent on dismembering
other women's warriors, heroes
all of them, across the seas.
Live and let live, I said to him,
and if you go falling for that flirt
Circe, I won't be responsible
for what I'll do. A girl deserves
some respect. I love you, he replies.
I know what he is. Yes, *is*, I say!
I may have my bad days, but on the whole
was is not a thought I'll entertain.
Talk of entertaining, had it up to here:
suitors eating us out of house and home,
pestering me with poems and with roses.
Well, I did seek comfort in Aurora, my maid,
but despite her young and sympathetic ear
she's proved a fickle, pouting creature,
and I begin to fear for my future peace
in the gloating eye of that serving man
she's taken to bringing up here of late.
I should have given her the diamonds
I suppose, but I thought she cared.
I did try raiding the cellar, to forget,
but wine was a cloud of visions raining
across the midnight silent room

so I'm abstaining, till he is home again.
It is so calm here, when no one's around:
the shuttle, click-clack, every afternoon,
my silent solitary virtue by night.
I miss him more than I could ever say.
If only my father-in-law lives long:
his breath keeps my bed cool and wide,
and shroud-weaving is my eternal occupation
while other voices carouse downstairs.
There are fates worse than pouring wine
down the eager throats of slim young men
with such human dreams: a woman at home,
or a scrap of power to clothe their naked lives.
Waiting makes me wise to the one I know I love:
I could no more forget than gouge out my eyes.
Odysseus will be back to spring his bow again.

The Siege of Weinsberg

Their king said we women could save ourselves
and anything else we were able to hold.
Then his forces would take control,
butcher our men, blaze the place to the ground.
Women got together, proposals were debated,
the liberals won it: we'd carry the men.
I'm all for solidarity, but count me out.

Just look at him, pudding-head, belching
by the fire; never touched me like someone
who knew what was where – who'd save him?
If I'm to carry anyone free, it would be
my Gertrude – she who knows how to slip
her fingers under my apron. We have learned
to dance together like sparks in the flames.

But the eyes of all the other wives: her cheeks,
branded. Nothing for it, but to chuck him
over my shoulder; hope, like a dove, in my hand.
Tomorrow she will sit, slender fingers in mine
and he will be suddenly deaf and blind.
We'll keep the fire in. Her face will glow.
Each man, however righteous, has his price.

To Angelica Kauffman's Self-portrait Hesitating Between the Arts of Music and Painting (1794)

That you had the choice at all is unexpected.
When we hesitated then, our choice tended
to be: to weed the beans or spread the dung?

and freely selecting a partner meant eloping.
But you stand tall in that white and flimsy gown
which no woman ever wore to get the dinner on

and you're gazing deep in a handsome matron's face.
She's trying to put your hand upon her breast
but looks like the moment for intimacy's passing.

'I love you still, but not in quite that way,'
your eyes are telling Music. Painting can't wait:
she's pointing out the path across the mountain

and your hand is already slipping into hers
but the route's in a mist. Though you hear birds
calling, you can only see to that first turning

and, though Painting has her romantic appeal,
can she bring the bacon home? Love may be real
but will you eat well? Passion is burning

but for how long? Be sure, for both their sakes
before you go eloping. Still, what it takes,
you've got. The proof is in the painting.

Wedded to Her Art

for Carrington (1893–1932)

For you, life was art: and how to conserve
time for it, a perpetual puzzle.

The Slade allowed you to draw women nude,
but only study men with their clothes on.
Then, even suffragettes pinned up their tresses,
but you and your friends dared bob off your hair,
along with your first names – just like the men:
Cézanne, Giotto: they didn't need one.

In any case, 'Dora' didn't suit you:
'the Cropheads', the gang that you belonged to.
In that group photo, your gaze is the firmest:
louche and lounging, your ankles revealed.
Out of the picture, the men from whom space
must be saved, to erect your own canvas.

You tried every amorous combination –
two loves at once to keep all heads swivelling
so no one was sure of taking control –
but what worked best was falling for Lytton
who loved boys to be boys, but in crophead you
found someone close enough to care for.

Here, you've painted the home you found him,
with your pair of swans, black lilies, floating;
the mill arch, an oval of outdrawn breath,
surprised by all those windows: room for art
no problem here, creative souls sheltered
by roof tiles bright as Uccello oranges.

Your mountain landscapes, posed like nubile girls,
grew later. Henrietta Bingham too,
who came to be drawn. Then drew you, to bed.
The sex worked best of all with her, you said.
Your standing female nude, she still walks tall.
Her love didn't last. Your work reveals all.

The 'YouWe' Portrait

'Darling Heart, we are not an "affair" are we –
We are husband and wife.' (Gluck, the artist, writing
to her lover, Mrs Nesta Obermer, 1936/7)

They're familiar enough. We've seen them in a bar:
the married woman with her bleached, permed hair,
the stunning butch she encounters there.
They find true love, in the front of her car

and fate's on their side, the husband's away.
Then follows the tale we're not told, but tell:
the all-night, the passion we know so well –
that never-so-alive feel, the following day.

That perfume some would call impossibility
permeates the greatest love they've ever known.
That list of excuses keeping her at home,
edited, reads: fear – financial instability.

So who could blame a butch if she gave her aching heart
to some lonely dog-lover, caring and sincere,
and clinched it dancing, murmuring in her ear,
then kissed so deep, to show they'd never part?

This is hardly the story which Gluck intended
to be perceived in her greatest work of art
which records, instead, the moment when the heart
is most alive. The story's happily ended

so why not leave it there? The dawn is glowing
on Nesta's face; two heads in round accord,
Gluck's cheek so close to hers. Oh they adored
for seven wild years. Which wasn't bad going.

Venice

*(on reading Margaret Forster's
biography of Daphne du Maurier)*

It was not a destination you ever recommended.

If pressed, you would deny you'd made the visit
and that the light seduced you,
the buoyant, expansive light.

No, you never had lounged in a gondola
dabbling your fingers into the lagoon
and no such signorina ever serenaded you.

That woman on the terrace of the San Marco café
was not you at all. As for her companion,
she was no Venetian: too delicate, too fair.

Cairo, you said, you yearned to visit,
and your husband's work took you to Egypt.
But the famous bazaar felt as dull as Borough Market.

The post was bad, but your letters finally arrived.

'Venetian' was du Maurier family slang for 'lesbian'.

Portrait of the Actress as a Young Girl

When she painted you, you were just a child.
And yet, that purposeful chin in profile
does not seem like someone of twelve or ten
but seriously you: a moment when

already, you are focused on your art.
Absorbed in thought, you play your model part
dressed in pink and black, no smile, a sober face:
you know your future's in a different place.

It takes determination to embark
on that voyage of discovery in the dark.
Talent and charm are not always enough
but art calls, even when the going's tough.

Whether in paint or print, on stage or screen,
creating, we're alive. You knew that then.

Night Off

The bell. I watch her down the stairs.
Her slicked-back hair, the leather tie.

One look she gives me. What I am
she knows. I stare. I smoke. I wait.

Some guy hollering outside the door:
'All you girls need is a night with me.'

In here we're free. 'Are you a member?'
When women dare, a locked door opens.

She's there. I pull a Gitane from the pack.
Her flame flickers. 'Babe, wanna dance?'

'If this was really the only world,'
I whisper at her cheek. 'It is, it is.'

Mounting the staircase, I am Dietrich,
all satin, and here is Garbo at my side.

Elegy for a Friend
(for J.W.)

Twigs crunched underfoot,
as dykes in dark trousers
carried her wicker coffin
up the wood-vale hill.
Men, too, shared the bearing:
all were welcome, she'd said,
having had time to plan.

She believed in mingling
the disparate and the lonely
– who might have stood apart
in the women's walking group –
she inspired, unified, made us
laugh together. I never knew
anyone less judgemental.

At her birthday party,
she guffawed for England
at that 'sexy at sixty'
card I gave her. Age
didn't stop all that, she said:
just the spontaneous
afternoon tumble into bed.

Then came cancer drugs,
bloating, the wheelchair.
The walker – trim, rosy-cheeked –
submerged for ever. Her voice
remained: Northern, familiar,
kind words still alternating
with telling it like it was.

Like the death of Diana,
it should have changed us,
made us gentler to each other.
Her laughter should have
spread through the group,
like wind through wheat,
but since then, we've scattered.

I'm stumbling through fog
and such beacons are rarer.
She'd say: fresh fields
lie ahead. Pack the torch.
Pick up the phone.
That when people falter,
art keeps us going. Walk on.

« La très chère »

I learn of your death only from your ex,
many moons after you and she had sex,
but not long since your friendship had revived:
she thrusts a recent photo. So alive,
you're laughing, still so chic, so slim, although
you'd reached eighty, and hadn't long to go.

You once met de Beauvoir: through Violette,
who wrote of you and your great love. Who left.
Expelled from six schools for seducing girls,
giving them Sobranies, stroking their curls:
father beat you blue, when you were a child,
made you board at eight. No wonder you were wild.

Pure Parisian, in this season's colours,
silk patterned cravat, sharply creased trousers,
plucked pencilled eyebrows, blusher, foundation:
your androgyny caused a sensation.
At the time your lipstick and your trilby
inspired me to give you my gay virginity.

You'd vanish, to read Pavese for hours,
pick up your pastels to sketch fresh flowers.
Barbara Hepworth moved you to write
in purple ink. Bach helped you sleep at night.
An unashamed intellectual,
not just beautiful, but multilingual.

Amazed it's a third of a century
since you slid naked into bed with me:
if only I had seen you one last time
before you slipped beyond the sound of rhyme.
Now that I know you died alone in bed
I can't get your laughter out of my head.

« La très chère » is the start of Baudelaire's poem 'Les Bijoux'.

Bohemian Elegies

1 – Violette Leduc

No ground is gained without blisters forming.
For her the ascent took longer than most,
and yet she still filled her pen each morning.
Tears flooded her face, but she was engrossed
in being so honest, the details shocked
even allies who wanted her published,
knew sex between teenage girls would be blocked –
though Genet's rent-boys made him established.

Violette persisted. So did her mentor:
for fifteen years, de Beauvoir paid her bills.
When came the book the public first went for
each sou was repaid from the ringing tills,
but the real joy was that artistic success
could spring from a life that had been such a mess.

2 – Simone de Beauvoir

How close to home, her final resting-place:
this gulf in the ground, where she sat and stared
at Sartre's remaining atoms on earth.
Traffic still murmurs, now she's joined him there.

Myriad lipstick prints surround their names,
their dates enough to place them in our minds.
Three red roses crown this indifferent grave.
She is not here, but in our hearts and heads.

Her thoughts shoot between us, whether we know
it, whenever we break our silence to speak:
she chose free love, fresh projects, constant growth.

I cannot find her here in the gold-leaved ground
but her voice rings out in the cafés around
and where women campaign. She loved that sound.

3 – Susan Sontag

She is one of ours: told it like it is,
loved whom she chose, and wrote about the bed
along with all the rest she had to say.

Doubly, triply, Other – with de Beauvoir
in her head, and a woman in her arms,
the writer who brought Camp to academia,

no wonder she insisted they bury her here:
Paris, the shore where all the diverse dwell
when they've evaded whatever youthful hell

told them they were not, should not, could never;
must wear today's straitjacket forever
whatever the smell of changing weather.

Her eyes burned with fire. She was not easy
but left diaries where we can find our own
way to that America, once called home,

of Greenwich Village, and Martin Luther King,
of infinite horizons, and wide skies
where bold roads rolled on for a thousand miles.

4 – Vaslav Nijinsky

Nijinsky, life-size, sits in stone, costumed
and capped, a Petrushka ruff encircling
his shoulders, pensive as if in mourning,
eyes downcast on his feet forever fixed.
Faded pink roses languish in his lap.
Can some ancient fan – once tiny, entranced –
have tottered here, said with flowers, that his dance
still reverberates like a thunder clap?

We last longer in legend than in mind.
Since his last public leap, a hundred years
have passed. No one is left to shed real tears,
but some lithe young man must have come to find
an icon who blazed his way on to stage,
loved as he pleased, in the beautiful age.

5 – Henry Murger

He has the tallest monument of all:
a stone nymph scattering petals on his grave.
Though he died penniless in hospital
Le Figaro appealed, the public gave
profusely, so he stood out in Montmartre
in death as in life. *La Vie de Bohème*
let loose a dream – that freedom, love and art
are all we need. The young know this means them.

Yet whether, like him, we die at thirty-eight
or gaze, amazed, at the mirror's louche lies
down the free-fall decades, it's never too late
to retrieve our dreams from those attic skies.
Let our wild geese fly wherever they will.
The vines still flourish on the Paris hill.

Murger's novel, *Scènes de la Vie de Bohème*, first popularised
Parisian Bohemianism (and inspired the opera *La Bohème*).

3. love and loss

In Grandpa's Garden

Salt breeze gusts.
Their petals hold.

He likes to share them
when family arrive,

of whom I'm smallest,
have never smelt a rose.

His gardening gloves
bend one stem towards me.

Petals deep as eiderdown,
soft peach on my cheek,

a scent that takes my breath.
It's like sleeping in strawberries.

Granny's

It was a cabinet
of glass animals
I was trusted
to touch, in that
silent back room.

A china hen, chick,
chipped cockerel,
who shared her farming
childhood, when a pet lamb
followed her everywhere.

Loud coal shaken on a fire,
a scullery, oranges
in a cut-glass bowl,
two sought-after
fireside chairs. No sofa.

A bank sprinkled white
where she showed me
it was spring,
once every finger
touched a daisy each.

We'd hunt the tortoise:
Trotty's jaws snapped
devouring buttercups,
and going wild
at blackberry time.

It was a hubbub,
all talking at once.
A huge tabby cat,
George, on her knees.
Her royal blue dress,

it was soft, shapeless,
lovely to lean into,
no bra, no bone,
it was apple blossom
and a proper cuddle.

Her Victorian childhood:
a photo so like my face,
high-neck, gingham dress,
clutching a slate proclaiming
'I have made every attendance'.

Getting on with it
(for Aunty Lucy)

At fourteen, pupil-teacher,
liberty bodice, bluebell
cotton, classes of sixty,
she had the gift of laughter
and of laying down the law.
My great-aunt, always 'Anty'.

Harold Hollinrake, her beau,
arm in arm to the bandstand,
Sunday tea beside the park,
a rosy understanding
fixed in the photo he left
when Todmorden went to war.

Four days less fire, and he'd not
have been a memorial name.
She grew apple-faced, furball-
figured, acquired her double bed,
flirtation with that bus driver
of hazy marital status,

tooting when he passed her door.
With her dog Tinker, she made
the best of it, roamed Stoodley Pike,
explored the moors with her car,
niece, nephew, Sunday ices,
St Annes, Illuminations.

I knew her when she'd downed chalk,
passing round the biscuit tin,
always jolly as Gracie Fields,
once offered us the furniture:
'It'll all go on t'bonfire, lovey,
you know, when I'm gone.'

Cooking the Sunday Roast
(for Aunty Freda)

She parboils potatoes, drains them,
lid tight on, shaken up and down,
like pebbles in a drum.

King Edwards emerge flakey,
their edges blurred. Hot dripping
sizzles as it seizes them.

Washing up as she goes,
confides, 'I don't like that teapot
he brought home. Its spout's too thin.

I might drop it, accidentally.'
He's in the fruit cage, clipping.
Smoke rises from his pipe.

He'll carve the joint, make her laugh,
pour her sweet sherry. Tonight,
they'll watch *Poldark* together.

A knock at the door.
A tall blond hero, with Sunday papers:
Peter, still a handsome man.

Her face transforms,
with a laugh that swings. Her voice
jives in and out of his.

The unpeeled parsnips languish
on the table. A big band's
playing 'In the Mood'

as it did way back, when, yes, they
fell in love, but, no, they never...
Her fiancé, away at war,

wouldn't release her. It's forever
too late to resume this dance
except with her quickstep eyes.

Sad State of Affairs

One day my mother lost her lid:
in a rare rage she threw a pan
across the kitchen at the man
she really never should have wed.

He had mistresses. She had God.
'Your mother's mad!' he ranted then.
'Your father's not like other men.'
What marriage does to love seemed odd.

My Uncle's Grave

'You see to the flowers, I'll do the grass.'
Should I let her bend? Her rheumatic knee.
But her jaw is set, and we never argue.

Purple daisies round the edge of the vase:
she calls them civil servants – at four
they close. White lilac, marigolds,
pink petals, blue, all from the garden
he used to grow.

It's a ritual for the living.
In the centre, the full-blown rose.

Suddenly I see beneath the ground old bones
that were his shape. Rib cage like an ox,
big hands that teased prize chrysanthemums
out of moist earth.

He gave me that slap when I was sixteen
and I looked back, knowing, daring him,
but she saw it too. Then he left me alone,
this uncle whose kisses were always lip-kisses,
a man about whom my father had warned me.

At Christmas they were the jolliest couple:
she'd get Grab the Cork up and going,
he would open more Asti Spumante,
the foaming bottle overflowing.
On their sherry glasses, flamenco dancers
clicked their castanets at each other.

Her silver head bending, shears snip snip.
Sun in the trees. Blackbird, singing.
A distant plane overhead, off to Benidorm.

Family

I told them I was leaving to go to a wedding.
'On a Sunday evening?' asked Aunty Peggy
who'd never wed but lived cheerfully in sin.
'That's right,' I said. We all breathed slowly,
bloated on roast beef, carrots and broad beans,
potatoes – mash and roasted, Bisto onion gravy.
The dog climbed my leg, rubbed, all excited.
Puce as a dahlia, my father bellowed,
'I hope it's a man and a woman getting married!'

'It's Matt and Dave,' I said, 'they're really happy,
they've been together for seventeen years.'
'Well, I think that's lovely,' said Aunty Freda
in her Berkshire burr, collecting the dishes.
'Have you time for crumble before you go?'
Peggy enthused about her line-dancing classes,
run by a charming couple, Lulu and Sandra.
My father stood up and strode about the room,
saying nothing at all. Which was quite unknown.

Today, once he's hoisted into the wheelchair,
requests, desires, bubble out like a child's.
'Why don't we see Freda? Why doesn't Peggy phone?'
I'm supposed to humour him, say we'll go tomorrow.
He's the last one I've got. I take him in my arms,
repeat it gently: we've lost them, both of them,
but they loved his treats, the birthday champagne.
His red face falls. Then rises, when a half of Guinness
is proposed, and roast beef is on its way, puréed.

Speech

They are expecting me, you know,
on stage, at six, the radio theatre.
Find my lecture notes, then I'll be ready
to face the room, the audience
in five continents, the famous
introducer, whom you must know:
John Hum... Hom... Humphill...
I'd still like to go on *Mastermind*,
if only I could find the time.

I don't think much of this hotel.
Breakfast in bed is all very well
but I don't like those women,
their overalls, the plastic gloves.
It's so damned undignified. And why
do they all hail from African nations?
I'd rather have Sue, my secretary,
offering me my next cup of tea,
the sight of her mini-skirt cheers me up.

Is it lunchtime yet? I have to see the bursar.
Who's at the door? Is it the army?
Before we leave, do find my demob papers,
should be filed under D for Denmark.
They might accuse me of being a deserter,
then send me out to Afghanistan.
What's that? Why, I'm fifty-six of course.
Nearly ninety? You're quite deluded.
I don't *look* ninety. Well, so you say.

Are you *sure* that fifty's too old for the army?
Well, I must say that's a great relief.
Yes, certainly time for my after-lunch sleep.
But have you bought pyjamas? Mum could do
with new ones. I'll give you the money.
Christmas is coming, don't delay it longer.
And some for yourself. What *are* you wearing?
And for Sue, pick out a baby-doll nightie.
John's not a patch on Jack de Manio.

'Girl!'

He started when I really was
and too young to teach him better.
No one else would dare.

He bought me fort and doll's house,
read me Eliot and Rossetti:
taught me to touch-type, like him,

held a patient sheet of paper
to conceal my tapping fingers.
As a father, couldn't fault him

though 'girl' I still remained
until one day he no longer knew
what actual name he'd given me,

only that when I came
and bent to kiss his cheek, I was
one visitor worth smiling for.

Changing Room
(for Aunty Freda)

Undressing for my swim, I think of you –
and skinny me at ten, green school costume,
seeking vainly an absent cubicle,
stunned by your huge breasts, filling up the room:
no slithering tops under insecure towels,
simple as a sister, you tossed off clothes.
I felt so flat. I covered up so fast,
prayed not to grow such bazongas as those.

Your swimming days are gone; my shame is too.
If we could still stand naked, side by side
you'd see how the family form lives on.
All bodies bulge somewhere. You taught me pride.
However clever we are, you realised,
we are flesh first, and have no need to hide.

Last Wishes

(RIP Aunty Peggy)

This pot of ash. It doesn't feel like you
and yet these friends await your final twirl.
We're blessed by sun, and enjoying the view –
granite cliffs, sapphire sea – but miss the girl
you still were: breath of fresh air, such a laugh.
I can't avoid it. You've got to be scattered.
I aim for the waves, but some grits the path.
Then the wind changes and my face is splattered.

Swooping to my rescue, a sudden plane
darts like a Spitfire through the Cornish skies.
'Look! It's Martin!' Your Australian airman
gave you his wartime heart, to your surprise.
Recently, he'd stay up late, to flirt by phone,
and cruise this breeze again, with you alone.

Letting Go

1

'All those beads!' said the prize-winning carer.
'My niece would love to take a look at those!'

When you were *you*, you chose them daily:
real pearls, strings of shells, scarlet baubles,

hand-knitted dresses with Laura Ashley pinafores.
My fashion-free mother, you had your style.

Beads flee into that space beyond your reach
with your last bookcase, your seat in the choir.

You clutch your handbag close, Mini Cheddars
well-concealed, in case they confiscate them.

Your legs no longer work, bed their only comfort zone.
I'm reassured you still retain your righteous rage:

'Left for hours! – pad caked solid! – say you care?!'
We are told no one else in the nursing home complains.

So you let your faith go too. I run for the vicar
on Easter morning, and she brings you back belief

like a strayed balloon. Your mind, you say,
is like a pile of sand blowing away on the breeze.

'Are you my grandfather?' you ask me when alone.
'Where are we? Is this prison, museum, school?'

You request 'a rude song', with the door open wide,
to make sure we entertain everyone else inside.

Magically, your mind returns, takes time to say
that I've been a wonderful daughter. What a day.

Then when you choke, eating up your greens,
pneumonia moves in, your final friend.

Food and drink go next. Then speech.
You abandon words with a sigh of relief.

Finally you give up breathing. Experimentally.
Fifteen seconds. Then start again. For days.

Maybe it's the Mozart CDs which keep you going
or dancing round magnolia trees with Sister Morphine.

2

One day, the bars have vanished from your bed.
The dress you'd choose? It's blue, with beads to go.

Sometimes – they explain, now you can't say –
the dying prefer their family out the way.

I say my goodbyes and take the train home.
That afternoon they're on the phone.

The Historian's Timepiece

No one would buy it, this wristwatch.
Cheap to start with, its clear face
stained with sweat. It's losing time.
I visit the jeweller to get a new battery.
He offers to snip the strap off too.
But when I explain that it was my father's
(who would never replace it till it fell apart,
in a spirit of wartime make-do-and-mend)

he handles it with the reverence I felt
in the suddenly silent hospital room,
explaining that I would take care of it
now that you didn't need it any more:
you, who always kept track of time,
now being beyond its grasp.

Baby Bellowing

You told me once that when I cried
you would come and say, 'Shut up!'
in my face, which, surprised,
I would often do.

Social workers would have come running
if I'd tried this, my dear ranting father,
with the night noise of you.

When your bellowing woke me, I calmed
with soothing words, like my mother's to me.

Now just one baby bellows here. No one comes.

The Bereaved

It's too simple to say we are lepers.
It's a myth that bits drop off lepers
without warning. When the bereaved
burst, it's with sudden explosions,
both fire and rain. People cross the road,
postpone that visit they'd intended.

Everyone's opting to be online anyway,
where the contact is cleaner, no germs
exchanged, and the bereaved dare not
commit themselves to how it really is.
We're among those who lurk,
trying to learn life goes on.

At times we are perfectly ourselves:
remember to eat,
find ourselves laughing,
take a moment to ask after you.
We make donations,
put our affairs in order.

But when grief sticks to our skin
and the more we flick it off,
the more it multiplies, all you can do
is try simple kindness, cheese scones,
do as you would be done by,
listen, but not stay too long.

Veiled

Nothing is quite right
for you tonight:
this seat, the company,
the icy wind.

Is it the invalid
you've left at home
or something I said
or didn't say?

In the glare
of the gathering
you wrap your scarf
around you.

In the intimacy
of email
your robes fall
to the floor.

Clearing My Father's House

No one wants to know about the fireworks in his attic:
twenty years old, could explode in the eyes
of anyone brave enough to light them.
The solicitor says shift them. The council won't take them.
A YouTube film says drown them, but when they dry
in rotting rubbish, what about the methane?
If I throw them in the river, what about the fish?
My doctor says bury them: how will that make it better?

I'm paralysed by all this explosive anxiety
just as, fifty years ago, I froze at the sound
of rockets ricocheting through this bedroom wall.
He and she hurled bangers, pretending it was private.
Someone should have stopped lighting the fuses
but war was entrenched. No one knew how.

Selling the Family Home

1

'You must have so many memories.'
My head is crammed with archive boxes (full),
seven cupboards-full, six paraffin cans,
five filing cabinets, four reel-to-reel recorders,
three thousand books, which well-spoken dealers
pick at, pile in crates, leaving those the dead read
to be gobbled up by Recyclosaurus.

'Rows,' I say, 'When he was home, they argued.'
Then try to return dirty linen to the basket.
When he was out, she played the piano,
con brio, certainly, to concert standard.
On Saturdays, we'd hear him typing all day,
composing those two shelves of history.

2

There were plenty of words, not just written.
'Action stations!' to his toddler daughter.
'I want to resign!' boomed from the toilet.
'Come along Betty!' No one in sight.
'WIFE! What's for supper? Have you sewn the button on?'
'WIFE! Oughtn't you to be doing something?'
'Old Filthy!' (re Mozart, pinched from Amis).
'Rotten swindling cheat!' when she won at Scrabble.

'It's the artistic temperament,' she'd sigh.
'Oh God! Oh Christ!' 'Jim! No profanity!'
'I'm off for my post-prandial nap,

about to fall into a drunken stupor.'
As Aunty Peggy put it, to her crossword,
'There he goes, chuntering on again.'

3

This house has multiple identities:
once a family home, with Sixties decor,
each room colonised by the ageing author,
and his alter egos: eager host, would-be lover.
My bedroom stripped to make a parlour,
for entertaining with his latest partner.
This house ceased welcoming me long ago
except as a guest, with sherry and stories.

I echo my mother, who, waiting in the aisle,
thought: 'This man really doesn't know me.'
He was so busy trying to know himself:
not always at ease with what he found.
Yet there was still a lot of love between us:
you don't have to understand to love.

4

When the carer got his room, I reclaimed mine,
since the only stairs he'd climb again
were in his wandering mind. The tree is felled.
No more will I bomb him over the banisters
with rolled up army socks, torch for searchlight,
or light up the sky with Standard fireworks,
please to remember the fifth of November.
He won't be passing me more treacle toffee.

I sleep at last where I was conceived,
enjoying the holly trees' final days.
He'd let the garden go. Where my mother
read *Winnie the Pooh*, doing all the voices,
is a dandelion island, in a sea of earth.
I place my chair there. She doesn't appear.

5

When we die, we rot, and are mostly forgot.

6

Now that they've gone, I thought my work was done,
and I'd reclaim my life, but all moves on:
I've lost my holdall and my destination.
Friends grow fearful if I tell it like it is,
must share myself in manageable doses.
Exes rally round. My lover gets me
dancing to a live band of troubadours:
it's so joyous, kids climb in through windows.

My favourite actress, on top form, at the
National Theatre, thrills me. Art is the answer.
Matisse's sculpture, two women embracing,
one boyish from behind, full frontal, all woman.
Writing still might banish to the shadows
that grinning death's head licking at my face.

Unsaid

The stain on the chair –
      she didn't dare say
            she needed to go –

recalls pitted walls
      where plaster pustules
            continued to crumble,

the grate where new firewood
      heaped on old cinders
            grew ash deep as snow.

Those Arum lilies
      we'd send if and when...
            let's give them today.

Hands

I didn't know I had
petal-smooth hands

till yours grew veined
like leaves reversed.

I couldn't then envisage
anything worse.

But now I have your hands,
and your ashes feed the roses,

I do it too – grab eagerly
the bluebells still in reach today.

4. travelling on

Chez L'Emigrée à Londres

In this garden, every inch is filled;
each flower has companions,
the earth abounds with life.

Iron chairs on the terrace;
pen, paper, space to write,
a gossamer thread on a potted palm.

Leaves shift on the breeze, whisper sense
like an aunt with her arms round
a wayward child, spring afternoon.

How lucky she is to have this garden!
'Luck?' she says. 'You wouldn't believe
the work it takes to get it this way:

look how the figs swell green.
Rub your fingers on this oregano:
smell. Imagine you're in Provence.'

The birds migrate this way. One calls,
another, more: then all solo voices merge.
Magnolia explodes like fireworks on the Thames.

For Karen

In a world where spectacles were round,
fathers wore waistcoats
and this au pair was German, that one French,

there your godmother taught you
how to prepare the 'English tea' you gave us:
through a strainer into porcelain cups –
milk first, knobbly sugar later –
pastry fork, for melting chocolate fancies,
tiny, bright white, linen serviettes.

Once you indulged me with photo albums:
your childhood in Denmark,
the farmhouse you came from,
the wide doorways resting on whole tree trunks.
Mop-haired white-blonde kids
tricycling through sepia fields.

You never spoke of Nazis appearing overnight,
just of your sister, who got the Jews out,
on the night-boats that slipped to Sweden.

About suffering, you were silent.

When your daughter rebelled, you were bourgeoise,
haute. That supposed Sisley lurked on your wall,
near Algerian hangings, fuchsia, emerald, gold.
In art and instinct always international,
your carpets were Persian, your cigarettes
occasional, in silver goblet on marble-top table.

These are things you don't now remember.

A cloud of starlings swirls across the sky.
The mountains, where you skied, rise up behind us.
You still place kernels of apricots you've devoured
neatly together on the plate you stretch to reach.

Now We Are All Welcome at the Feast
(for Ingrid and Rosa's wedding day)

Love conquers all,
creates a herb garden
where mint, thyme, tarragon,
rosemary and coriander
flourish in Burgundy earth.

Love garnishes a kitchen
with pestle and mortar,
trays filled with *tomates farcies*,
courgettes garnies, and pans
of golden sauté potatoes.

Love produces the perfect menu.
Vegetable pâtés melt on the tongue,
our bread is wholegrain, our bowls full
of good things, to soothe the soul:
and there's raspberry tart to follow.

Love fills a room with laughter
whether twenty arrive for dinner
or just two, free to gaze
into each other's eyes
while soup simmers slowly.

Love leads us on
to wander arm in arm
by the long canal
where we lie at our ease
in the afternoon sun.

Love slips off our clothes
sends us racing in the lake,
with the barest of breeze
through the willow trees
and the vineyards beyond.

Purbeck Stone

Adamantine rocks
slice off like cheese,
crash to smithereens.
The path to the cove
a torrent stream where

Blue Lias reverts
to primeval mud.
Spiral ammonites
re-emerge through slime,
escargots in sediment

where we too will soon
abandon our bones
whole or in cinders
like those before us:
their laugh as raucous

whose moist hands delved
as deep in loving flesh;
who swam as naked,
playing like dolphins
in some secluded bay,

all sure that we live
with such intensity
so hip hip alive,
nothing came before us
or will drown us in dust.

Challenge

There is the rock. Volcanic grey it stands,
a fifteen-minute swim across the bay
with the group of women who meet each day:
first timers, repeat enthusiasts, old hands.
We plunge in together, but then we fan
out, as if it's each woman for herself.
Deep below, the pull of the ocean shelf.
I long to stop and sink. I know I can.

But then I remember a day in the park:
I'm small, at the top of a mountainous slide.
I'm only two. We are both terrified
by my firm decision to make my mark.
She's warm and smiling as she waits below.
Hot steel burns beneath me as I let go.

At the Turtle Café in Skala Eressos

Calm reigns here. Green gourds swell.
The Aeolian harp's hypnotic cadence
sings from the fingers of this dark-haired girl.

The sea believes her, goes on breathing.
Here I am at the edge of the horizon:
there is no temptation to wander further.

Feet plant themselves in volcanic sand,
and wait for streaming sun to gold the water
then leave the stage to the slither moon.

I have to rebuild after the storm,
creating a shack from driftwood:
no one else is coming to do it

though dancers may shimmy out of the dark
and draw me in, smiling. I might find
new talents, learn to play the mandolin.

.

Our Walk at Alciston

This is the path we know so well:
past the horse with the hopeful eyes
who crunches the greener grass you offer
across the fence. Beyond, the tall hedges,
the winter woodpiles, Old Postman's Cottage
where two women loved, before our time.
The stonking geese still strut their stuff:
the bantams banter, scatter and return.

The doors to the tithe barn are shut
tight as eyes in the early hours
and on the former mounting stone
fresh eggs for sale, from hens grown free.
The breeze in these ancient trees
is just how you breathe in your sleep.
We avoid the mud like dancers
placing their toes with precision.

At the top, offered two paths,
we take neither the right nor the left,
but climb our own way up to where
the fields spread, umber and green
and gold, swaying like a sea. Here
where we have basked in heat,
chosen to climb further, or to clear
the air, here you will always be.

Perfect would never do for us.
Sometimes I drift, a balloon off course,
forget to follow the sun, am full of fear.
Or you parachute on to some far plain
and don't know when you'll be home.
Yet when we linger to kiss in clover,
spring still swells, vast and moist,
in this, the harvest time of our lives.

Excursion to Évora

White houses spare their residents from roasting,
yellow-rimmed windows discourage lizards,
she tells me, this young graduate, forced to
apply her Art History to the tourist boom.
Lemon and orange trees fruit near entrances,
the scent of citrus deters mosquitos.
They work on farms – cork and cattle – and live
in layers, Roman columns in cobbled patios,
workshops squeezed between aqueduct arches.

Where the Inquisition tortured, they now hang
modern painting, free to view on Sundays.
Where martyrs were flamed, visitors seek sun,
enjoy custard tarts at café tables.
She shows me a restaurant where I'll lunch well.
This oval marble fountain is still encircled
by solid seating, where poets may compose
beneath the crown inserted on its summit
when plague drove the Court to its refuge here.

To the cathedral, they added crenellations,
a watch tower, archers at the ready.
This Virgin, fingering her swollen belly,
drew women to pray for safe deliveries.
The Franciscans walled a chapel
with bones and skulls, all sizes, infants',
but the rich never got the message:
thrusting madly gilded shrines
either side of this simple nave.

Gold over blue is exquisite, she says:
this gold-leaf carving, the azure *azulejos*,
are the pride of Portugal, the home she loves
though rising rents expel her to the suburbs.
A wise salamander, ever adaptable,
spending her days sharing her passions,
she points, on the motorway back to Lisbon,
to storks, now nesting in pylons all year,
since winter grew warm as Africa here.

azulejos – tiles

When cities are centred around people

we won't need squares, only circles,
intersecting like Olympic rings,
streets round which kids canter, racing
laughing wheelchair users on wide pavements.
In centrifugal libraries, like minds will gather,
artists arrange easels in a horseshoe,
the model reclining in her chosen curve.
Poets will cavort in spiral stanzas,
acrobats loop the loop in amphitheatres,
guitarists jam all day in domed studios,
while engineers win spherical medallions
for making homes of eco-elegance
which export all around the world outside.

Awakening

I wake on a beach. It's warm. A flamingo
is paddling in the shallows and pecking
the sand with an air of abandon. The sun
slides like a gleaming dinner plate up
a cloudless sky and my toes twitch
with anticipation. Later we decamp
to the beach bar, the flamingo and I,
where those I love most are all waiting,
each as they were in their prime.
My father, in straw trilby and baggy shorts,
proffering endless champagne.
My favourite mentor, brown as golden syrup,
debating mai '68 with my Parisian ex-lover
from years ago. My long-embraced sweetheart,
beaming, takes me openly in her arms
and they all cheer, even my mother,
with God now talking love, not conformity
in her ear. My most feminist ex-lover
is making the man who wanted to marry me
laugh like a cowbell. Women dance
thigh to thigh. When my aunts jolly up
in sleeveless frocks, proposing a swim,
the Wonder-dog is lolloping through the waves
so they scamper, giggling, after him,
and my favourite actress, a glass of fizz
in her hand, is deep in conversation
about Natalie Barney, her literary salon,
with my almost-sister, who made the journey
as her soon-to-be wife is quite recovered.
To the scent of jasmine, a sax starts playing,
and, swift as whippets, we all twist again.

Acknowledgements

I am very grateful to Tzeli Hadjidimitriou for generously giving permission to reproduce one of her 'Dancing Nudes' photographs on the book cover. More details of Tzeli's work, as a photographer, film-maker and author of various books, including *A Girl's Guide to Lesbos*, may be found on her website www.odoiporikon.com. I've been so lucky in Helen Sandler, the most patient, honest, diplomatic, and meticulous of editors, whose enthusiasm is inspiring.

Thanks are due to the following poetry publishers. 'Bridges' (1989) and 'Not Over Yet' (1993) featured in the Kent & Sussex Poetry Society prizewinners' anthologies. The *Western Mail* and *The North* published 'At the Opera' after it won a prize in the Cardiff International Competition in 1992. Along with 'Chess Game' and 'Penelope Confides In Her Loom', it was published in Brighton Poets' *Ice on the Wing* in 1993. 'Ten' was commended in the Margot Jane Memorial Prize competition anthology in 1994 and was republished, with 'Chess Game', in *We want to tell you how...* (Paradise Press, 2018). 'To Angelica Kauffman's Self-portrait...' appeared in *The Interpreter's House* in 2015. 'The Historian's Timepiece' was published in *Artemis* in 2018. The quote from Gluck is reprinted with kind permission, from p.126 of Diana Souhami's *Gluck: Her Biography* (Pandora 1988, republished by Quercus 2013).

Among poets, I am particularly grateful to Jackie Wills (first met through Brighton Poets) and Mimi Khalvati (first met as an Arvon tutor) for their perceptive encouragement and constructive criticism, both in the 1990s and more recently. I'm also grateful for helpful feedback in recent years to Ruth O'Callaghan, Hannah Lowe, Michael Laskey, Anne-Marie Fyfe, Cahal Dallat and Anny Knight; members of Brighton Poetry Stanzas, Lewes Literature Live workshops, the Gay Authors Workshop, the Colander group and Second Light. Some poems here have also benefited from feedback from past members of Brighton Poets, and from other Arvon course tutors, including Jackie Kay and Simon Armitage. My thanks also to Amanda, Ann, Ingrid, Jane, Jill, Lace, Mary, Meg and Susan, all enthusiastic readers of poetry, whose encouragement has been much appreciated; to Lesley Wood, whose gift of the photo-book led to 'Dining Out', and to Lydia Haward, whose suggestion for a poem about jewellery resulted in 'Letting Go'.